FIRE ENGINES

by Anne Rockwell

A TRUMPET CLUB SPECIAL EDITION

Published by The Trumpet Club
1540 Broadway, New York, New York 10036

Copyright © 1986 by Anne Rockwell

ISBN: 0-440-84480-0

This edition published by arrangement
with Dutton Children's Books, a division
of Penguin Books USA Inc.

Editor: Ann Durell   Designer: Isabel Warren-Lynch

Printed in the United States of America
October 1991

10 9 8 7 6
UPC

I like fire engines.

I like to watch the fire fighters

wash and polish their fire engines.

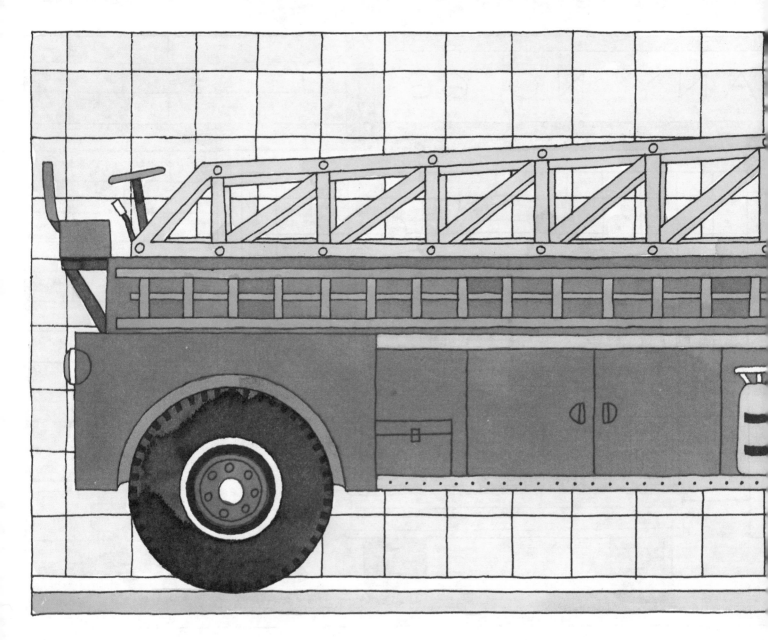

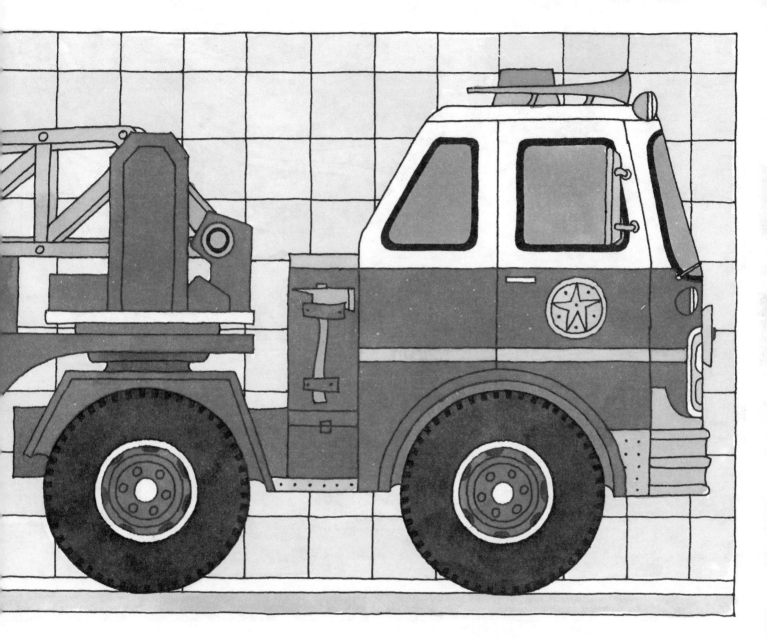

Ladder trucks have long ladders.

Motors raise the ladders high in the air.

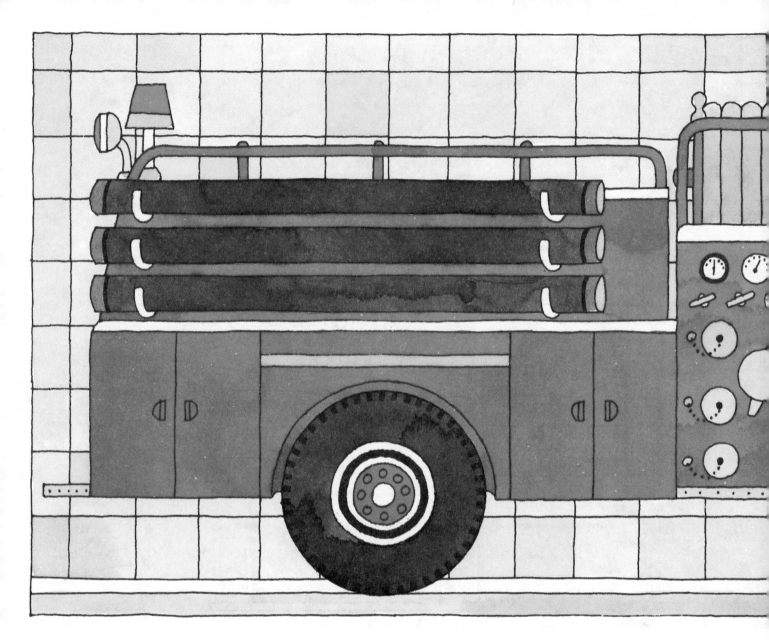

Pumper trucks have hoses and pumps.

Water is pumped from a hydrant.

Hoses spray the water on fires.

Some fire engines have pumps

and hoses and ladders.

A firehouse ambulance comes
to help anyone who is hurt in a fire.

The fire chief drives a bright red car
and wears a white helmet and coat.

Some fire engines are yellow,

but I like red ones best.

Some fire engines are boats that
put out fires on ships and docks.

They spray water from the harbor.

Fire fighters are brave and strong.

Their fire engines are shiny and beautiful.

I want to be a fire fighter and drive
a real fire engine when I grow up.